W9-BAY-209

CORNERSTONES OF FREEDOM™

SEPTEMBER 11
We Will Never Forget

BY PETER BENOIT

CHILDREN'S PRESS®
An Imprint of Scholastic Inc.
New York   Toronto   London   Auckland   Sydney
Mexico City   New Delhi   Hong Kong
Danbury, Connecticut

BRINGING HISTORY to LIFE

Content Consultant:
Christopher Gelpi, PhD
Professor of History
Duke University, Charlotte, NC

Library of Congress Cataloging-in-Publication Data

Benoit, Peter, 1955–
    September 11 We will never forget / by Peter Benoit.
        p. cm.—(Cornerstones of freedom)
    Includes bibliographical references and index.
    ISBN-13: 978-0-531-25040-2 (lib. bdg.)   ISBN-10: 0-531-25040-7 (lib. bdg.)
    ISBN-13: 978-0-531-26565-9 (pbk.)   ISBN-10: 0-531-26565-X (pbk.)
    1. September 11 Terrorist Attacks, 2001—Juvenile literature. 2.
Terrorism—United States—Juvenile literature. I. Title. II. Series.
    HV6432.7.B427 2011b
    973.931—dc22   9194   2011009586

4 5 6 7 8 9 10 R 21 20 19 18 17 16 15 14 13 12

Photographs © 2012: Alamy Images: 44 (Scott J. Ferrell/Congressional
Quarterly), 5 bottom, 27 bottom (Richard Levine), 50 (Craig Ruttle); AP
Images: 2, 3 (Peter J. Eckel), 14, 52 (FBI), 15 (Prakash Hatvalne), 55 (Don
Heupel), 6 (Marty Lederhandler), 28 (Brennan Linsley), 51, 56 top (Doug
Mills), 7 (Masaaki Noda/KYODO), 16 (Joel Page), 48 (Matt Rourke), 4 top,
13 (Tech. Sgt. Cedric H. Rudisill/Department of Defense), 33 (Rahimullah
Yousafzai), 17 top, 56 bottom; REX USA/BEImages: 30, 57; Clifford Oliver
Photography/www.cliffordoliverphotography.com: 64; Contact Press
Images/Lori Grinker/© 2001: cover; Corbis Images: 24 (Shaun Heasley),
49 (Brendan McDermid/Reuters), 22 (Mark Peterson), 27 top, 59 top (Ron
Sachs); Getty Images: 47 (Henny Ray Abrams/AFP), 34 (Patrick Aventurier/
Gamma-Rapho), 45 (Dennis Brack/Bloomberg), 21 (Timothy A. Clary/AFP),
25 (Ed Darack), 18 (Douglas Graham/Roll Call), 38, 54 (Chris Hondros), 40
(Stephen Jaffe/AFP), 11 (Todd Maisel/NY Daily News Archive), 23, 58 right
(Thomas Monaster/NY Daily News Archive), 8, 53, 58 left (Lyle Owerko),
39 (Spencer Platt), 4 bottom, 10, 17 bottom (Mario Tama); Magnum
Photos/Paul Fusco: 36; Media Bakery: 32; NEWSCOM/Mark Wilson/UPI:
46; Polaris Images/Dbox: back cover; Reuters: 5 top, 31 (Department of
Justice), 41 (Hyungwon Kang), 26 (Win McNamee); ShutterStock, Inc./
Carolina K. Smith, M.D.: 43.

Did you know that studying history can be fun?

BRING HISTORY TO LIFE by becoming a history investigator. Examine the evidence (primary and secondary source materials); cross-examine the people and witnesses. Take a look at what was happening at the time—but be careful! What happened years ago might suddenly become incredibly interesting and change the way you think!

Contents

Mayhem in Manhattan

New Yorkers watch as the World Trade Center is attacked.

The morning of September 11, 2001, was calm and peaceful in New York City. People hurried to work under cloudless skies. They were ready to face the challenges of a new day. Meanwhile, in Boston, Massachusetts,

NEARLY 3,000 PEOPLE, FROM MORE THAN

American Airlines Flight 11 lifted off at 7:59 a.m. Flight 11 was a passenger jet bound for Los Angeles, California.

At 8:46 a.m., Flight 11 crashed into the North Tower of the World Trade Center (WTC) in Lower Manhattan. It was traveling at almost 500 miles (805 kilometers) per hour. People on the sidewalk hundreds of feet below did not understand what they had just witnessed. They did not know that a tragic series of events had been set in motion at 8:14 a.m. Egyptian terrorist Mohamed Atta had risen from his seat in business class and **hijacked** the jet with four other terrorists. Atta took over the plane's controls and turned its path toward New York. A tragedy that would raise questions and reshape U.S. history was about to unfold.

Smoke billows from the North Tower after the crash of American Airlines Flight 11.

CHAPTER 1

ATTACKED!

The South Tower erupts in flames after being hit by United Airlines Flight 175.

SEVENTEEN MINUTES AFTER the North Tower was hit, a second plane slammed into the South Tower of the World Trade Center. It was traveling at almost 600 mph (966 kph). United Airlines Flight 175 was hijacked by five terrorists. They were led by Marwan al-Shehhi of the United Arab Emirates. News reports flashed across the world's televisions, computers, and radios. America's worst fears had come true. The horrible crashes were not accidents. They were carefully planned terrorist attacks against the United States.

Some people were able to evacuate the World Trade Center after the towers were hit.

Terror in the Streets

Fires raged and gray smoke clouds billowed up from the Twin Towers. Crowds gathered on the sidewalks below. Terrified people struggled to escape from the towers. New York City firefighters responded within minutes of the North Tower attack. They set up command headquarters in the lobby of the North Tower. Then they began working to rescue the 17,400 people inside the towers.

Heat and smoke made escape almost impossible for the people located above the points where the jets hit. Less than 10 percent of the people above these points of impact survived. Ninety percent of the people on lower floors made their way to safety.

Some people trapped on the upper floors jumped from the blazing towers. They fell hundreds of feet onto rooftops and sidewalks below. Staircases were jammed with fleeing victims. There was not enough room for everyone to leave at once. Many people scrambled to the roof. They thought they would be rescued by helicopters. The doors to the roof were locked. The heat and smoke made helicopter rescue too dangerous. People reached

Firefighters rescue a survivor from the World Trade Center.

for their phones and called loved ones. They hoped to make sense of the terrible event or simply say a final good-bye.

The Ripple Widens

The nation watched the horrors unfold as a third jet crashed into the Pentagon, the center of national defense, in Virginia at 9:37 a.m. Five terrorists had forced their way into the cockpit of American Airlines Flight 77 about 30 minutes after its departure from Washington Dulles International Airport. The hijackers were led by Hani Hanjour of Saudi Arabia.

The hijackers had difficulty at the airport's security checkpoint when they attempted to board. They set off metal detectors. Their bags were rechecked. The five men were eventually allowed to board the plane. They carried **box cutters** and knives with them. They and 184 other people lay dead at the Pentagon less than two hours later.

A FIRSTHAND LOOK AT
THE NORTH TOWER COLLAPSE

The attacks on September 11, known simply as 9/11, were witnessed in person by thousands of people on their way to work. Some had video recorders. Of course, the news media arrived at the site within minutes. As a result, there are countless primary source images of the 9/11 tragedy. See page 60 for a link to watch a video of the North Tower's collapse online.

Rescue workers and Federal Bureau of Investigation agents inspect the damage to the Pentagon.

Revolt in the Sky

The hijackings weren't over. United Airlines Flight 93, left Newark, New Jersey, at 8:42 a.m. headed for San Francisco, California. Four hijackers stormed the cockpit 45 minutes after takeoff. Ziad Jarrah was the Lebanese leader of the group and a pilot. He took control of the Boeing 757. Many people believe he planned to crash the plane into the U.S. Capitol or the White House in Washington, D.C.

Flight 93 burned a section of forest when it crashed near Shanksville, Pennsylvania.

The passengers thought the terrorists had a bomb. The people on board the plane learned from cell phone calls that other hijackings had occurred earlier. The hijackers only had control of the plane for about 30 minutes. Then the brave passengers stormed the cockpit where Jarrah was manning the controls. Terrorists held the door shut.

Jarrah rolled the jet side to side to try to throw the passengers off balance. It did not work. It seemed that the passengers would soon break into the cockpit. Jarrah deliberately crashed the jet into a field near Shanksville, Pennsylvania, at 10:03 a.m. The crash killed everyone on board.

The 110-story South Tower had collapsed four minutes earlier. It had been badly damaged by the impact of Flight 175 and the fire. The North Tower fell at 10:28 a.m. **Debris** rained down on the nearby 7 World Trade Center. The 47-story tower was set on fire. By 5:21 p.m., that building also lay in ruins.

A VIEW FROM ABROAD

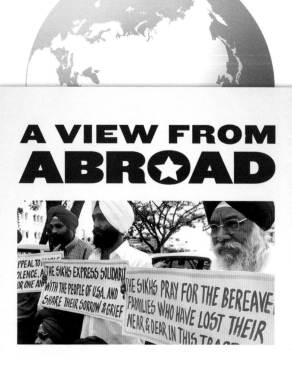

The victims of the tower attacks were from more than 90 nations. It is not surprising that the 9/11 tragedy generated reactions from around the world. Even some nations and groups normally against U.S. policies expressed outrage at the actions of the terrorists. Libyan leader Muammar Qaddafi called the attacks "horrifying." Palestinian activist Hanan Ashrawi promised, "We will do everything we can to help." Other groups supported the attacks. The Islamic extremist group Hamas praised the killing of Americans. An official Iraqi statement claimed, "The American cowboys are reaping the fruit of their crimes against humanity."

Portland, Maine, police chief Michael Chitwood displays a photo of two men believed to be 9/11 terrorists, entering the city's airport.

Identifying the Terrorists

The identities of the 19 hijackers and details of the September 11 attack plans were discovered within hours. Mohamed Atta was the leader of the operation. He had flown from Portland, Maine, to Boston, Massachusetts, before boarding American Airlines Flight 11. His luggage held the hijackers' identities and details of their plans, backgrounds, and motives. It never left Portland. The Federal Bureau of Investigation (FBI) revealed that the hijackers had ties to the militant Islamist group **al-Qaeda** and its commander Osama bin Laden.

Many people believed that sorting through the many connections between the terrorists and radical Islam was not the most urgent need. It was more important to deal with the confusion and fears of U.S. citizens and the health and safety of the survivors.

A firefighter is overcome with emotion during rescue efforts on the day of the attacks in New York.

SPOTLIGHT ON

Osama bin Laden

Osama bin Laden was born into a wealthy and devout Islamic Saudi family in 1957. He attended King Abdulaziz University in Jeddah, Saudi Arabia. There, he became fascinated by the interpretation of the **Quran** and in the concept of **jihad**. After college, bin Laden fought against the Soviet invasion of Afghanistan. In 1988, he formed the extremist group al-Qaeda. In 2001, bin Laden and his associates carried out their horrific plot against the United States. He was killed in 2011 by a team of U.S. Navy SEALs.

CHAPTER 2

A NATION RESPONDS

President George W. Bush delivers a speech to Congress following the September 11 attacks.

THE RESPONSE TO THE

September 11 attacks took several forms. Emergency personnel worked to evacuate the buildings. They rescued people who were trapped. This short-term response required several agencies to work together. They ran into many problems. U.S. president George W. Bush announced a global "war on terror." He hoped to remove any governments giving aid and shelter to al-Qaeda. Governments around the world **denounced** the terrorists. They spoke out in support of the United States. Iraq stood almost alone in criticizing the United States. It blamed the attacks on U.S. policies. New York City mayor Rudy Giuliani provided strong leadership to calm the nervous city.

Those Who Rose to the Challenge

The Fire Department of New York (FDNY) and New York City Police Department (NYPD) were the first to respond. Several thousand people were still in the towers. It would be necessary to safely and quickly evacuate the buildings. The fires were fed by jet fuel. The structural soundness of the buildings became the main concern as the fires burned. The towers' stairways had not been designed for mass evacuation. Heat and smoke limited how much time helicopters had to evacuate people from the top floors. Nearly everyone was killed at the points of impact. A financial services firm located in the impact zone of the North Tower lost 658 employees when the first plane crashed.

Doctors, emergency medical technicians (EMTs), and nurses treated the wounded and brought supplies from hospitals nearby. The Coast Guard and more than 100 local boats rushed to Lower Manhattan to help with evacuation. The Civil Air Patrol flew in blood donations. All other nonmilitary flights had been grounded. One

U.S. National Guardsmen march into the devastated area around the World Trade Center early on September 12, 2001.

million people had been evacuated by late afternoon. Two thousand of them had been injured in the attacks. The National Guard sent more than 2,500 members to the scene. They helped frightened citizens find missing friends and family. They sorted through debris and assisted in rescue efforts with U.S. Marine Corps troops at their side. The U.S. Navy sent a hospital ship to Manhattan to provide meals and shelter for rescue workers. Selfless heroism was the order of the day.

Communication Problems

The rescue operation was slowed down by communication difficulties that cost time and lives. The National Military Command Center worked to organize all of the response efforts during the first hour after the attacks. But it failed to include the Federal Aviation Administration's (FAA) air traffic control center. The center had important information about the hijacking.

Emergency responders at ground level faced a number of problems. Fire department chiefs had established special areas near the towers. Firefighters were supposed to stop there first for instructions. But many bypassed the areas and reported directly to the

Firefighters make their way through dust- and smoke-filled streets to the World Trade Center.

A firefighter is helped to safety after being trapped in the basement of the South Tower when it collapsed.

towers without a plan. Commanders on-site had to quickly make plans instead. Radio communication failed. The system that allowed emergency workers inside the towers to communicate with commanders outside had been damaged by the impacts. Firefighters were unable to plan their work with other emergency workers. Workers in the North Tower were not aware that the South Tower had collapsed. They never heard evacuation orders. Three hundred and forty-three firefighters lost their lives when the towers collapsed.

YESTERDAY'S HEADLINES

Why were NYPD officers evacuated from the towers in time, while FDNY personnel remained and lost their lives? In May 2004, the *Dallas Morning News* reported the findings of a commission that studied the reason. The study determined that poor communications were largely to blame. The paper reported, "Firefighters operating in the North Tower were unaware that the South Tower, which was hit second, collapsed. Without that knowledge . . . the firefighters 'lacked a uniform sense of urgency in their evacuation. . . . We didn't have a lot of information coming in,' Deputy Assistant Fire Chief Joseph Pfeifer told the commission. . . . 'It was impossible to know how much damage was done on the upper floors, whether the stairwells were intact or not.'"

The collapse of the South Tower made it necessary to move the FDNY's command post. This added to the confusion. Debris from the collapsing North Tower killed FDNY chief Peter Ganci. This made it even more difficult to coordinate responses. The debris also fell on the nearby 7 World Trade Center. This damaged the building and set it on fire. The Office of Emergency Management was in charge of coordinating the responses of police and firefighters. It had been located at 7 World Trade Center. They were forced to evacuate the building. Rescue workers were left without a central headquarters. People ran from the dust clouds and toxic fumes. But escape did not come easily.

The Larger Stage

Government officials and agencies responded in a number of ways. Civilian aircraft were grounded across the country if they were not involved with relief efforts. In later days, President Bush's war against terrorism placed trade **embargoes** and took military action against nations that supported terrorists. The United States led a military coalition made up of many countries against the government of Afghanistan. The Afghan government was controlled by a group called the Taliban. The Taliban had aided al-Qaeda. The coalition invaded Afghanistan and overthrew the Taliban.

Marines patrol a mountainside in Afghanistan's Kunar Province.

Tom Ridge is sworn in as the first director of Homeland Security.

President Bush also promised increased **surveillance** and greater sharing of **intelligence**. This involved a massive reorganization of government. The Department of Homeland Security was established. New laws gave the department extraordinary access to law enforcement information. Plans were put in place for dealing with both biological (harmful bacteria and viruses) and nuclear warfare. Border security was tightened. Many pilots were allowed to carry weapons. The Homeland Security Council was established to advise the president on national safety.

On October 26, 2001, the USA Patriot Act became law. It gave police investigators the right to search e-mail. It also gave them access to telephone, financial, and medical records in cases of suspected terrorism. Critics claimed that privacy abuses would become common. They believed that Americans' most basic civil freedoms would be taken away.

TODAY'S PERSPECTIVE

Many citizens were living in fear when President Bush signed the USA Patriot Act into law 45 days after the September 11 attacks. Reports of foreign al-Qaeda terrorist groups began to surface. Americans feared that these groups might also exist closer to home. Supporters of the Patriot Act felt that no price was too high to pay for the nation's safety. But critics feared that privacy and liberty had been traded for peace of mind. As a result, there has been a strong negative reaction to the Patriot Act.

A protestor holds a sign during a rally against the Patriot Act.

YOU ARE UNDER SURVEILLANCE

PEOPLE FOR THE AMERICAN WAY

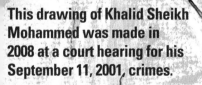

CHAPTER 3

THE FACE OF TERROR

This drawing of Khalid Sheikh Mohammed was made in 2008 at a court hearing for his September 11, 2001, crimes.

THE POWERS GRANTED TO LAW enforcement officers by the Patriot Act seemed to confirm Americans' fears in the weeks following September 11. Investigators discovered that al-Qaeda had several "cells" of followers around the world. Those groups communicated with one another. Investigations also revealed that the September 11 attacks had been planned for years. Khalid Sheikh Mohammed was a Pakistani associate of bin Laden. He was the "principal architect of the 9/11 attacks" according to an official report. Al-Qaeda members had studied U.S. airport security and flight schedules. Al-Qaeda hijackers had trained and become certified commercial pilots in the United States. Investigators were also becoming aware of people much closer to home who were sympathetic to al-Qaeda.

SPOTLIGHT ON

Khalid Sheikh Mohammed

Khalid Sheikh Mohammed had been involved in terrorist activities in the United States and other countries before 9/11. He helped pay for the bombing of the World Trade Center in 1993. Seven people were killed and more than 1,000 were injured. In 1994, he plotted to place bombs on one dozen commercial jets flying between the United States and the Philippines. By mid-1996, he was laying the groundwork for the attacks of September 11, 2001. He was captured in Pakistan in 2003. He remains in U.S. custody awaiting trial for his crimes.

Anthrax

A week after the 9/11 attacks, letters containing deadly **anthrax spores** were mailed to several major news outlets in New York City. On October 9, two more anthrax-laced letters were mailed to U.S. senators Tom Daschle and Patrick Leahy. Panic swept through the country. Americans wondered if this was a second stage of attacks on America. Al-Qaeda was initially blamed for the letters. Hijacker Mohamed Atta was known to have had anthrax lesions on his hands in the weeks before the 9/11 attacks.

Blame for the letters was eventually placed on a worker in a U.S. government research lab. But the evidence that he sent the letters is not conclusive.

Fears remained. The anthrax letters were mailed within the United States one week after the 19 terrorist hijackers

Senator Tom Daschle from South Dakota was one of the people to receive an anthrax letter.

died in the 9/11 attacks. Another frightening possibility existed if other people had mailed the letters. There could be people sympathetic to the hijackers' cause living in the United States. This atmosphere of hysteria allowed President Bush to sign the Patriot Act into law.

Security at airports was increased. Armed air marshals were authorized to travel on flights within the United States to discourage hijackings. Government personnel at airports had to be careful not to single out Middle Eastern–looking people at security checks. This is called

TODAY'S PERSPECTIVE

The 9/11 hijackers were all similar in age and ethnicity. It seemed reasonable to many people to focus security measures on those with similar physical characteristics. But civil rights groups have suggested that the practice of profiling is not effective in stopping terrorism. Many terrorists do not fit the young, Arab male profile. Critics argue that the practice may even increase hate crimes and anti-American beliefs in the Arab-American community. Opinion polls of Americans still swing sharply in favor of profiling after terror events.

ethnic profiling. Ethnic profiling became a controversial issue in the months following the 9/11 attacks.

Al-Qaeda

The FBI began gathering evidence against the hijackers, bin Laden, and al-Qaeda in the days following September 11. They discovered that Khalid Sheikh Mohammed had earlier studied mechanical engineering in North Carolina. He earned a degree in 1986. He and bin Laden both hated the United States because of U.S policies in the Middle East. The two believed the policies were anti-Arab. Investigation into the group that hijacked Flight 77 revealed several startling facts. Hanjour had been educated at the

Osama bin Laden talks to reporters in Afghanistan in 1998.

University of Arizona. He had trained to be a pilot in
Scottsdale, Arizona, during the 1990s. He earned his
FAA commercial pilot's license in April 1999. He received
further flight training in New Jersey and Maryland in
2001. Between those years, he had failed to become a
commercial pilot for Saudi Arabian Airlines. This made

Afghan fighters stand among the remains of an al-Qaeda training camp after helping U.S. troops take control of the area.

him angry and frustrated. He found a home for his rage in militant Islamism. He traveled to Afghanistan and met Osama bin Laden. Hanjour was handpicked for the terrorist plot bin Laden was planning.

A FIRSTHAND LOOK AT
TERRORIST TRAINING

A video of al-Qaeda militants training in Afghanistan before the September 11 attacks has been made public. It shows soldiers training with guns and explosives and working together as small teams on Afghanistan's rough terrain. See page 60 for a link to watch the video online.

The FBI also learned that many members of al-Qaeda were training in Afghanistan. U.S. military forces destroyed al-Qaeda training camps and killed a majority of the group's leadership when they invaded Afghanistan. The Taliban was removed from power. But bin Laden was not found until 2011. U.S. forces discovered him hiding in a compound in Pakistan. Bin Laden was shot and killed when a team of U.S. Navy SEALs attacked the compound.

American intelligence agencies also connected the hijackers to a group of radical Islamist students in Germany. Mohamed Atta, Marwan al-Shehhi, and Ziad Jarrah became close friends there. They also met Ramzi bin al-Shibh. He was supposed to have been the 20th hijacker. He did not participate because he was refused documents he needed to enter the United States. The four met almost daily to discuss their anti-American opinions. They also traveled to Afghanistan and swore loyalty to bin Laden.

CHAPTER 4

SWIFT ACTION

A girl visits a 9/11 memorial in New York City.

THE IMPACT OF THE SEPTEMBER 11 attacks was too vast to be measured. The attacks had a devastating effect on the U.S. and world economies for years to come. Thousands of New York City residents, firefighters, police, and rescue personnel suffer ill health because of the toxic debris and fumes they were exposed to at the WTC site. It will be decades before the full impact of the attacks can be determined.

One World Financial Center was one of the nearby buildings damaged during the September 11 attacks.

The Human Cost

The attacks rocked the financial world in the United States and abroad. The New York Stock Exchange closed for one week. The market dropped drastically when it reopened. It set a record for the largest one-day decline. About 430,000 jobs were lost in New York. About 18,000 small businesses were ruined or had to relocate. Millions of feet of office space were damaged or destroyed. The air travel and tourism industries were crippled.

The effect of the attacks on the health of those nearest the tragedy may be one of the most distressing results of 9/11. Much of the debris at Ground Zero, the name given to the site of the WTC attacks, contained harmful chemicals. Recovery workers exposed to the toxins have suffered diseases such as cancer and breathing disorders. Many other New Yorkers have also experienced symptoms of ill health because of the toxic air they breathed daily while near Ground Zero.

The United States was battered, but not beaten. The U.S. government and ordinary citizens launched a series of programs to prevent future terrorist attacks. They also paid tribute to the thousands who died on 9/11.

A cleanup worker takes a breathing test almost a year after 9/11.

Homeland Security

The Department of Homeland Security was created by the Homeland Security Act of 2002. This marked a turning point in America's handling of terrorist threats. The department has three main goals. First, it prevents terrorist attacks. It also prevents people from bringing chemical, biological, and nuclear materials into the United States. Finally, it secures the safety of important buildings, bridges, tunnels, resources, and leaders.

One of the department's methods of operation is monitoring activity on the Internet. This function of the department is called cybersecurity. Workers monitor terrorists who use online message

The Homeland Security Act

The Homeland Security Act of 2002 was another response to the 9/11 attacks. Effective November 25, 2002, the act created the U.S. Department of Homeland Security headed by a secretary of homeland security. The secretary is also a member of the president's cabinet of advisers. The act calls for many new measures to fight terrorism. They include obtaining and analyzing intelligence information, and sharing that information among local, state, and government agencies. The act also outlines plans to combat chemical and biological terrorist threats and ways to secure borders, ports, and terminals.

The National Cybersecurity and Communications Integration Center is located in Arlington, Virginia, outside Washington, D.C.

boards and chat rooms to plan attacks and recruit new members. Terrorist Web sites also serve as training grounds. They show how to build bombs, fire missiles, and fight U.S. soldiers. People suspected of running the sites can be charged with crimes and tried in court.

A FIRSTHAND LOOK AT
CYBERSECURITY

A panel of cyberspace experts from the U.S. government and the technology industry studied security in cyberspace and made numerous recommendations to President Barack Obama. Their report claims that cyberspace is one of the nation's biggest security threats. See page 60 for a link to read an article about cybersecurity online.

Aviation Security

The 9/11 attacks resulted in improved security at U.S. airports. Security also increased at other transportation terminals and ports of entry into the country. The U.S. government established the Transportation Security Administration (TSA) in November 2001 to handle passenger and baggage screenings and security at U.S. airports. Private companies hired by airports or airlines had previously done the screening.

The TSA established a long list of items that could not be carried onto airplanes. These included box cutters, scissors, guns, fireworks, spray paints, many types of chemicals, and even sporting goods such as baseball bats, hockey sticks, and golf clubs. Check *www.tsa.gov/travelers/airtravel/prohibited/permitted-prohibited-items.shtm* for a complete list.

The TSA also employs armed federal air marshals who travel with passengers and flight crew members. They detect and stop acts of terrorism directed at planes, airports, and passengers. The TSA trains pilots how to use handguns. It also offers self-defense instruction to airplane crew members.

A Welcome Exchange of Information

One reason for the attacks cited by many experts was the failure of various U.S. organizations to share intelligence information each had collected.

TSA agents search luggage they consider suspicious.

U.S. attorney general John Ashcroft (left), Homeland Security director Tom Ridge (center), and FBI director Robert Mueller (right) attend a Senate hearing regarding Bush's war on terrorism.

U.S. authorities were aware of many of the hijackers well before 9/11. Rumors of a possible attack on the World Trade Center had been circulating for months.

U.S. authorities recognized the dangers created by not sharing information. A report issued in 2008 by the U.S. Director of National Intelligence compared the trading of information among terrorists with those of U.S. agencies: "Our adversaries [enemies]. . . freely communicate, obtain training, share information on tactics, gather intelligence on potential targets, and spread propaganda. . . . In this post-9/11 world, intelligence must move faster and leverage all sources of intelligence information."

Information sharing became the new goal in the months after 9/11. The Department of Homeland Security was put in charge of more than 20 intelligence-collecting agencies. These agencies and departments were given access to each other's information. One of the largest collections is the Secret Internet Protocol

A September 12, 2001, editorial in the *New York Times* identified one of America's most immediate challenges: fighting terrorism. It stated that the nation "must also begin the urgent work of determining how an open and democratic society can better defend itself. . . . The best defense against terrorism is good, timely intelligence. The Central Intelligence Agency and other organizations have enjoyed some quiet victories, but much more must be done to try to infiltrate terrorist groups and to track their activities and communications. No one suggests this is easy or inexpensive work, but . . . the nation should know more about terror networks and their plots."

The National Counterterrorism Center collects, analyzes, and shares information used in counterterrorism.

Router Network. The network was established in the 1990s. It is used by the Departments of State and Defense. The network includes secret documents and communications that help identify terrorist threats.

The National Counterterrorism Center in McLean, Virginia, was established in 2003. It is the home of the many intelligence-sharing groups working to fight terrorist threats. More than 30 intelligence, military, law enforcement, and homeland security organizations are housed together. The center is a model of information sharing. About 3,000 federal and independent employees work there. They review more than 5,000 pieces of terrorist-related information gathered from intelligence organizations each day.

"If You See Something, Say Something"

Many Americans lived in fear of further terrorist attacks in the weeks following 9/11. In 2002, the New York Metropolitan Transportation Authority (MTA) decided to empower residents with a security-awareness campaign. The campaign was aimed at preventing terrorist plots. The MTA oversees the city's subways, buses, bridges, and tunnels. It encouraged New Yorkers to report suspicious activity or unattended packages

Security of the MTA in New York was increased immediately after the terrorist attacks, with the National Guard joining MTA police.

wherever they were seen. A campaign using the slogan "If You See Something, Say Something" appeared in subway cars, buses, and trains.

The response from the public was overwhelming. The events of 9/11 had made most people feel a need to help fight terrorism. The MTA's program was a simple yet effective way of getting the public involved in its own security. The program's hotline received more than 16,000 calls in 2009.

On May 1, 2010, several New York City street vendors noticed a smoking car in the heart of Times Square.

The success of If You See Something, Say Something led to a nationwide campaign.

For safety, officers disarming the car bomb in Times Square, New York City, wore special bomb suits.

Times Square is one of the city's busiest areas. The vendors called the hotline. Police quickly responded. They found gasoline, propane, and a bomb in the vehicle. Law enforcement teams quickly found the terrorist responsible for the car bomb. He was trying to flee the United States on a flight to the United Arab Emirates. The bomb did not go off. No one was injured. The MTA's program had proven its importance in combating terrorism.

Honoring the Fallen

About 3,000 people were killed on 9/11. Hundreds more have died from illnesses related to their heroic rescue attempts. The U.S. government and private citizens are making sure that those heroes will never be forgotten.

Construction on the September 11 Memorial took place throughout 2010 and 2011.

The National September 11 Memorial & Museum at the World Trade Center has been established to honor the dead and respect the historic site of America's tragic loss. The memorial was opened on September 11, 2011. It consists of two huge pools with the nation's largest human-made waterfalls located on the site between the two fallen towers. The names of those who died at the WTC, the Pentagon, and in Pennsylvania aboard Flight 93 appear around the edges of the memorial pools. The museum presents a gallery that tells the story of 9/11. It contains artifacts, photographs, narratives, oral histories, and multimedia displays. Visitors can also view the "Last Column." It is a massive steel beam that survived from one of the towers in the attack.

The Pentagon Memorial is located near the Pentagon. It serves as a tribute to the 184 people who lost their lives in the building and on Flight 77. The Flight 93 National Memorial is in Stonycreek Township, Pennsylvania. It is about 2 miles (3.2 km) from the crash site. The memorial honors the 40 men and women who died stopping the terrorists from reaching their intended target.

The President's Call to Action

President George W. Bush addressed the nation in a televised speech on the evening of September 11, 2001. He concluded his brief message by saying, "This is a day when all Americans from every walk of life unite in our resolve for justice and peace. America has stood down enemies before, and we will do so this time. None of us will ever forget this day. Yet, we go forward to defend freedom and all that is good and just in our world."

President Bush addresses the nation on September 11, 2001.

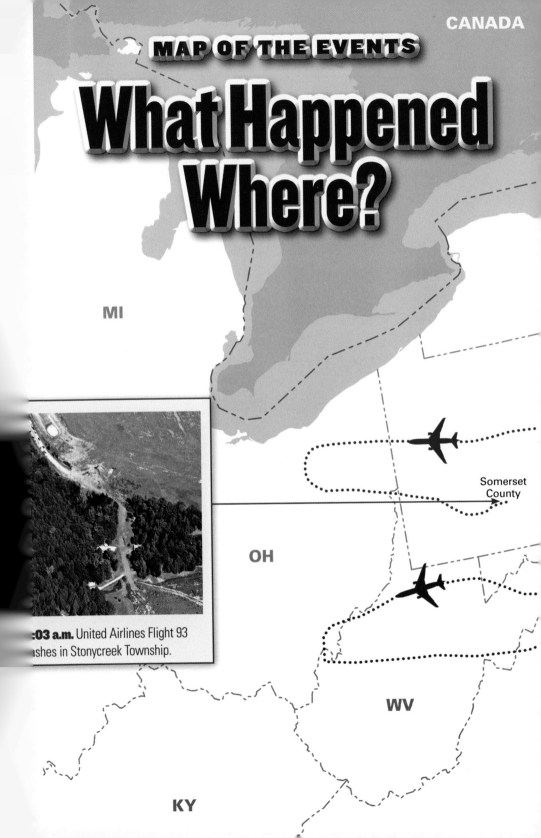

CANADA

What Happened Where?

MI

Somerset
County

OH

:03 a.m. United Airlines Flight 93
ashes in Stonycreek Township.

WV

KY

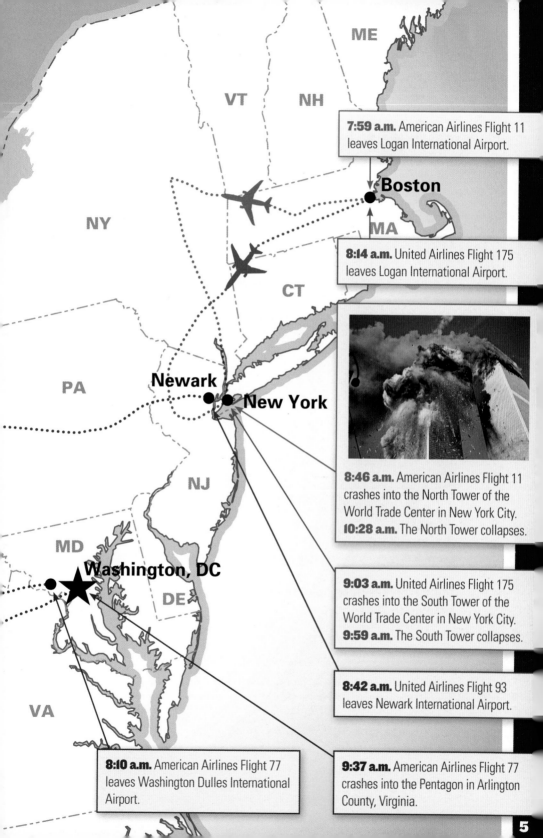

ME

VT   **NH**

7:59 a.m. American Airlines Flight 11 leaves Logan International Airport.

Boston

NY

MA

8:14 a.m. United Airlines Flight 175 leaves Logan International Airport.

CT

PA

Newark

New York

8:46 a.m. American Airlines Flight 11 crashes into the North Tower of the World Trade Center in New York City. **10:28 a.m.** The North Tower collapses.

NJ

9:03 a.m. United Airlines Flight 175 crashes into the South Tower of the World Trade Center in New York City. **9:59 a.m.** The South Tower collapses.

MD

Washington, DC

DE

8:42 a.m. United Airlines Flight 93 leaves Newark International Airport.

VA

8:10 a.m. American Airlines Flight 77 leaves Washington Dulles International Airport.

9:37 a.m. American Airlines Flight 77 crashes into the Pentagon in Arlington County, Virginia.

A Question of Balance

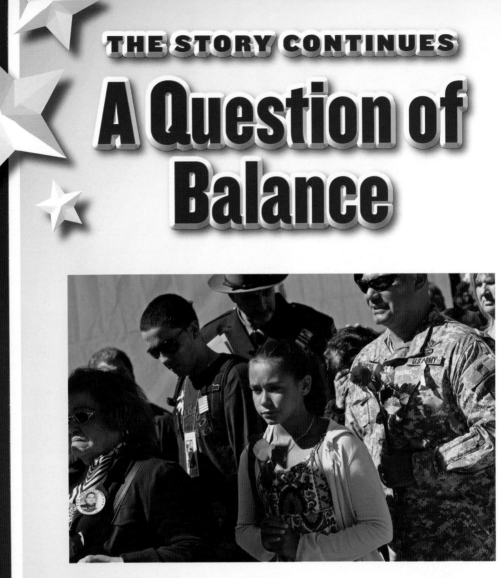

Memorial services have taken place every year following the attacks in 2001.

The numerous laws and acts established to fight terrorism remain one of the most important results of the 9/11 attacks. Many people believe the increased governmental authority challenges basic rights of privacy guaranteed to all U.S. citizens. The Declaration of Independence argued for each citizen's "**unalienable** rights."

The events of 9/11 have brought the need for safety and the right to personal freedom into conflict with one another. The USA Patriot Act allows the government to monitor what Americans read, search their property and computers, review medical and financial records, and search and seize items from people's homes without consent. The greatness of the United States will one day be measured by its ability to solve the dilemmas created by 9/11.

Many U.S. citizens are opposed to the Patriot Act.

Patrick Leahy (1940–), a U.S. senator from Vermont (1975–present) and chairman of the Senate Judiciary Committee (2007–present). He was a target of the 2001 anthrax letter attacks.

Rudy Giuliani (1944–), served as mayor of New York City from 1994 to 2001. His strong leadership after 9/11 helped unite the city and made him a nationally recognized politician.

Peter Ganci (1946–2001), was chief of the Fire Department of New York and was among the 343 FDNY firefighters who died on September 11.

President George W. Bush

George W. Bush (1946–), served as the 43rd president of the United States from 2001 to 2009. He was the driving force behind the reorganization of government that created the Department of Homeland Security.

Tom Daschle (1947–), a U.S. senator from South Dakota (1987–2005) and Senate majority leader (2001–2003). In 2001, he was the target of an anthrax letter attack.

Osama bin Laden

Osama bin Laden (1957– 2011), a member of a prominent Saudi family and founder of al-Qaeda. He encouraged Khalid Sheikh Mohammed to carry out the 9/11 attacks. In 2011, U.S. forces discovered him hiding in Pakistan. Soon afterward, he was attacked and killed by a team of U.S. Navy SEALs.

Khalid Sheikh Mohammed (1964 or 1965?–), a Pakistani and confidant of Osama bin Laden's who masterminded the 9/11 attacks. He is currently in U.S. custody awaiting trial.

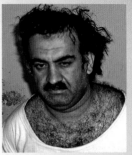

Khalid Sheikh Mohammed

Mohamed Atta (1968–2001), an Egyptian, was the leader of the 19 terrorists and the pilot of the hijacked American Airlines Flight 11, which he crashed into the side of the WTC's North Tower.

Hani Hanjour (1972–2001), from Saudi Arabia, was the hijacker-pilot of American Airlines Flight 77, which he crashed into the Pentagon.

Ramzi bin al-Shibh (1972–), a Yemeni extremist and prominent member of the Hamburg, Germany, cell. He was to have been the 20th hijacker but was denied a visa to the United States.

Ziad Jarrah (1975–2001), from Lebanon, was a prominent member of the Hamburg, Germany, cell. He hijacked and piloted United Airlines Flight 93, which he crashed near Shanksville, Pennsylvania, in response to the passenger uprising.

Marwan al-Shehhi (1978–2001), a student from the United Arab Emirates and a key member of the Hamburg, Germany, cell in the al-Qaeda terrorist network. He piloted the hijacked United Airlines Flight 175 and crashed it into the WTC's South Tower.

TIMELINE

1996	1998–2001	2001	September 11, 2001
Khalid Sheikh Mohammed develops 9/11 plot	Hamburg, Germany, terrorist cell becomes the nucleus of the 9/11 attack team	Hijacker-pilots complete flight training and certification in the United States	Day of the attack; massive evacuation and rescue program unfolds

2003	2008
National Counterterrorism Center opens in McLean, Virginia	Pentagon Memorial honoring the 184 victims aboard American Airlines Flight 77 and at the Pentagon is dedicated

September 18, 2001	October 7, 2001	October 26, 2001	November 25, 2002
Anthrax letter attacks begin	President George W. Bush announces war on terrorism; Afghanistan War begins	USA Patriot Act signed into law	Department of Homeland Security is created

May 2, 2011	September 11, 2011
Osama bin Laden is killed by U.S. Navy SEALs in Pakistan	Phase one of the Flight 93 National Memorial in Shanksville, Pennsylvania, is dedicated; National 9/11 Memorial is dedicated in New York City

DID YOU KNOW...

That the **USA Patriot Act** is an acronym that stands for
Uniting and **S**trengthening **A**merica by
Providing **A**ppropriate **T**ools **R**equired to **I**ntercept and **O**bstruct **T**errorism.

LIVING HISTORY

Primary sources provide firsthand evidence about a topic. Witnesses to a historical event create primary sources. They include autobiographies, newspaper reports of the time, oral histories, photographs, and memoirs. A secondary source analyzes primary sources, and is one step or more removed from the event. Secondary sources include textbooks, encyclopedias, and commentaries.

The Collapse of the North Tower Thousands of people witnessed the 9/11 attacks in person. Some had video recorders, and the news media arrived on site in a matter of minutes. As a result, a detailed visual archive of the 9/11 tragedies is available to us. Here is one example: *www.history.com/topics/world-trade-center /videos#collapse-of-the-north-tower*

Cybersecurity A newspaper article and link to a report from U.S. government officials and the technology industry about monitoring possible terrorist attacks can be found at *www.nytimes. com/2008/12/09/technology/09security.html*

Rescue and Survival Despite the FDNY's heavy losses in the WTC rescue effort, there were some miraculous stories of survival. Listen to one fire chief who survived the collapse of the North Tower. He was inside when the building fell around him. You can see the collapse and its aftermath, and hear his words at *www.history.com/topics /world-trade-center/videos#911-rescue-and-survival*

Terrorists in Training Before the 9/11 attacks, al-Qaeda militants trained in Afghanistan. A video that shows soldiers training with firearms and explosives can be seen at *www.youtube.com /watch?v=p04lptVK-7M&feature=player_embedded#at=11*

RESOURCES

Books

Frank, Mitch. *Understanding September 11th: Answering Questions About the Attacks on America*. New York: Viking Juvenile, 2002.

Gerdes, Louise I. *9/11*. San Diego: Greenhaven Press, 2010.

Kowalski, Kathiann M. *A Pro/Con Look at Homeland Security: Safety vs. Liberty After 9/11*. Berkeley Heights, NJ: Enslow Publishing, 2008.

Miller, Mara. *Remembering September 11, 2001: What We Know Now*. Berkeley Heights, NJ: Enslow Publishing, 2010.

New York Times. *The New York Times: A Nation Challenged: A Visual History of 9/11 and Its Aftermath: Young Readers Edition*. New York: Scholastic Reference, 2002.

Roleff, Tamara L. *America Under Attack: Primary Sources*. San Diego: Lucent, 2002.

Santella, Andrew. *September 11, 2001*. New York: Children's Press, 2007.

Stewart, Gail B. *America Under Attack: September 11, 2001*. San Diego: Lucent, 2002.

Web Sites

History.com—9/11 Attacks: 102 Minutes That Changed America
www.history.com/topics/world-trade-center/interactives /witness-to-911#/home/
Check out complete video footage of the WTC and Pentagon attacks, as well as photos, interviews, and timelines.

New York Times—Times Topics
http://topics.nytimes.com/top/reference/timestopics/organizations/a /al_qaeda/index.html
Read the New York Times' archives on the radical Islamist terrorist organization al-Qaeda.

GLOSSARY

al-Qaeda (al-KY-duh or al-KAI-duh) a radical Islamist terrorist group formerly headed by Osama bin Laden

anthrax spores (AN-thraks SPORZ) bacteria that cause a potentially lethal infectious disease

box cutters (BOKS KUHT-uhrz) razor blades with handles, used by terrorists as weapons

debris (duh-BREE) wreckage and scattered remains

denounced (di-NOUNSD) condemned openly as being evil

embargoes (em-BAR-goz) official orders forbidding something from happening, especially trade

hijacked (HYE-jakd) forced an airplane pilot to surrender control of the plane

intelligence (in-TEL-uh-junce) information concerning an enemy or possible enemy

jihad (gee-HOD) a holy war waged on behalf of Islam as a religious duty

Quran (kor-AN) the holy book of Islam

surveillance (sur-VALE-ence) close watch kept over someone or a group

unalienable (uhn-ALE-ee-uhn-uh-buhl) unable to be given, or taken, away

INDEX

Page numbers in *italics* indicate illustrations.

ABOUT THE AUTHOR

Peter Benoit is a graduate of Skidmore College in Saratoga Springs, New York, with a degree in mathematics. He has been a tutor and educator for many years, and has written more than two dozen books for Children's Press. He has written about ecosystems, disasters, and Native Americans, among other topics. He is also the author of more than 2,000 poems. He is a historical reenactor and reads extensively about American history. As a native of New York State, he knows many families whose lives have been touched by the 9/11 tragedies. He hopes this book brings them some small bit of peace and greater understanding.